Tableau Classroom Drama Activities

Active Learning via Silent, Still Images

Rosalind M. Flynn

ISBN-13: 978-1544017532
ISBN-10: 1544017537

Table of Contents

The Purpose of this Book

Tableau (tab-BLOW) is the theatrical technique in which actors freeze in poses that create a picture of one significant moment in the play.

♦ *When the curtain rises and all the actors onstage are frozen in poses that create a compelling stage picture, that's a Tableau.*

♦ *When two scenes that occur in different locales are on stage at the same time and the actors in one scene freeze in poses while the actors in the other scene talk and move. The frozen scene is a Tableau.*

Stillness and silence are the hallmarks of Tableau, so it's understandable why this drama strategy appeals to teachers for classroom use! But to really get the most out of Tableau work that enhances the reading of a story, novel, play, or text book, student actors have to do deeper reading, thinking, and rehearsing.

♦ They need to work like actors who explore the text and experiment with a variety of alternatives before they choose their final poses.

♦ They need to practice focus and commitment so that they pose with expression on their faces and energy in their bodies.

♦ The best Tableaux show evidence of comprehension of text combined with strong acting skills.

♦ The best Tableaux go far beyond mere silence and stillness.

Detailed Descriptions. Most instructions to teachers for using drama in the classroom are overwhelmingly minimal:

♦ "Have students act out...."

♦ "Place the students in roles...."

♦ "Cast the students as the characters...."

Successful use of drama strategies such as Tableau requires more than a one-sentence instruction. This guide provides teachers a detailed approach to leading student actors in the creation of effective, productive, artistic, and meaningful use of Tableau drama strategies.

About the Author

 Rosalind M. Flynn has led Tableau work with students and teachers since 1995. In years of teacher workshops and classroom residencies, she has sharpened her approach to productive student involvement in classroom drama strategies. The book she co-authored with Lenore Blank Kelner, *A Dramatic Approach to Reading Comprehension* (Heinemann 2006), offers detailed descriptions of the drama strategies Tableau and Human Slide Shows. The contents of this new book reflect the continued practice of this classroom drama work.

Arts Integration. Rosalind focuses her classroom work on the principles of arts integration. Curriculum content provides the material for the drama; the tools and skills of theatre increase the discipline and the quality of the work. The solid integration of content and theatre leads to productive and meaningful work. This book's goal is to share with teachers as precisely as possible Rosalind's approach to Tableau work. It's a practical "how to" guide with photos, examples, and resources.

Resources. Other resources for this work may be found on Rosalind's web site **RosalindFlynn.com** and her blog— **DramaticApproachesToTeaching.com**. Visit **Vimeo.com** and search for her name to find videos of the Tableau work and more.

Rosalind holds a PhD in Curriculum and Instruction. She is the head of the M.A. in Theatre Education at The Catholic University of America in Washington, DC. and a national teaching artist for The John F. Kennedy Center for the Performing Arts.

Tableau as a Classroom Drama Strategy

Creating a Tableau helps students make mental images. Making strong mental images is a skill that helps readers increase their understanding of a text that they read. Good readers are able to make a "mental movie" that plays in their minds as they read and visualize what the words on the page describe. Planning, rehearsing, and presenting Tableaux—taking words from a page and depicting them on the "stage"—aid in the creation of strong mental images.

It's not enough to tell students to freeze and hold a pose. When students engage in the kind of thinking that actors and directors do to create stage pictures that are visually compelling, they also engage more fully with the subject matter of their Tableau. They examine the text more carefully, make deeper inferences, and explore alternative ways to communicate what they are reading and learning with their faces and bodies.

In the process, students also learn about the art form of theatre. Students who know and practice the theatre skills that contribute to strong Tableau work experience, in a small way, both the creativity and discipline required of actors as they work together to rehearse and then share a presentation.

Leading Effective Tableau Work

The following directions serve as a lesson plan (or plans) to help teachers and leaders introduce and involve students in Tableau work that is worthwhile and meaningful. The step-by-step approach described here is one way to introduce this drama strategy to students. The overall goal is to increase the likelihood that they will participate productively in frozen, silent, concentrated posing that contributes to greater understanding of curriculum content. Students should also enjoy being actively involved in a creative process that keeps them engaged, motivated, and in control of their bodies and voices.

       Begin with Tableau Basics. Before using Tableau in a curriculum context, it's best to teach the basics of the drama strategy with a compelling imaginary circumstance. The intentions of the introductory process described on the following pages are to 1.) capture students' imaginations with a dramatic situation they can envision, 2.) involve the whole group simultaneously, 3.) give students practice in creating a Tableau, and 4.) coach students to revise and create an energetic and effective Tableau.

Introducing Tableau to Students

Whole Group Tableau

Begin by engaging __all__ students simultaneously in agreeing to pretend to be in a specific situation and react accordingly.

1. Arrange students seated in their desks, in chairs, or on the floor so that they are all facing in the same direction—towards you.

2. Explain that the upcoming activity involves **drama**. This means that they will have to agree to pretend that they are in a different circumstance (not in a classroom) and that they may even play different characters. Secure the students agreement to pretend—to engage in drama.

3. Describe a particular fictional circumstance (preferably a dramatic one!) and setting that they might find themselves in.
   Example: *"Would you agree to pretend that the setting for our drama is the schoolyard and while we are out there, we sight an alien space ship?"*

4. Discuss with students the possible feelings and reactions of people having this experience: *"If this really, truly was happening, think about how you would feel. Raise your hand if you can give me one adjective to describe how you would feel."* (Tell students that it's okay if they have the same adjective/feeling as another student. Ask students to share their adjectives. Limiting them to just one word allows for a more rapid sharing of thoughts.)

5. Point out to students that the kind of thinking they are currently doing is precisely the kind of thinking that actors have to do. They must imagine that they are in a particular pretend situation and then figure out how their characters would likely feel and react.

6. Then ask the students to agree to pretend that a photographer snaps a photo of them in that circumstance: *"Would you now also agree to pretend that a photographer just happens to be there in the schoolyard and takes a photo of the moment you spot that alien spaceship?"* (This

notion of a photo helps beginning student actors prepare for the silence and stillness aspects of Tableau.)

7. Explain how you will **cue** the students to strike and hold their poses: *"I will say "Action – 2 – 3 - Freeze!" You freeze in your pose and hold it until I say "Relax."*
   (Note: Eventually, you all will want to improve this first Tableau by allowing students to leave the confines of their seats, but for now, do not give them permission to do so unless a student asks specifically.)

8. Identify a **focal point**—in this case, the imagined alien space ship—so that all student actors will share the same focus. In a classroom, this focal point or **point of concentration** could be a sign on the wall, a screen, a bulletin board, or anything above eye level in the direction that students are facing.

9. **Teaching Tip**: You may need to remind students that they are playing themselves in this drama activity and thus, they have no weapons. This reminder usually eliminates ideas of posing with guns before they happen.

10. Once you feel that the students are ready, cue them with *"Action – 2 – 3 - Freeze!"* (You may want to actually take a photo of this first draft of the Tableau. Viewing it later will allow student to self-critique.)

11. View the Tableau for about 10 seconds and then call *"Relax."*

Discuss the Whole Group Tableau

In that first draft of the Tableau, the students usually participate well and enthusiastically, but they often remain seated. Compliment them for their cooperation. But, just like actors who rehearse and rehearse their scenes, most groups of students need to work on increasing the dramatic value of the Tableau. Here's how to **coach students towards increased dramatic value in their Tableau**:

1. Explain to students that the drama activity they just participated in is called a Tableau—a frozen "picture" that actors make with their bodies.

2. Invite students to consider the "photo" they just created. Ask or remind students what photographers may do to people in their photographs who do not look too interesting—They crop them out!

3. Hold a discussion with students about what makes a photograph of people, and therefore a Tableau, visually compelling—**energy in their bodies, expression in their faces**.

4. Explain that to avoid getting "cropped out," there are some adjustments that student actors can make. Share the following dramatic coaching points:

Dramatic Coaching Points

Describe and demonstrate (or choose a student to demonstrate) how actors create a more interesting Tableau by…

1. …using strong **energy** in their bodies and strong facial **expressions**. Demonstrate the difference between a low energy pose and facial expression and a high-energy version of the same reaction.

2. …incorporating **levels**—posing close to the floor, mid-level, or reaching higher.
   In a visually compelling Tableau, actors pose in variety of levels:
   a. **low** to the ground (stooping, kneeling, lying)
   b. **medium** level (bending, leaning, sitting)
   c. **high** level (standing, reaching, stretching)

3. …**interacting** with one another to increase the dramatic effect of the Tableau.

Tableau Excellence

Share the **Tableau Excellence chart** on the opposite page. Project it using a document camera or reproduce the list below on a chart or chalkboard.

Tableau Excellence

Actors...

...remain <u>still</u> or <u>frozen</u>.

...remain <u>silent</u>.

...pose with <u>energy</u>.

...pose with <u>expression</u>.

...keep their <u>concentration</u>.

...pose at different <u>levels</u>.

...pose with an <u>audience</u> in mind.

...choose poses that communicate the <u>mood</u> of the dramatized moment.

Revise the Same Whole Group Tableau

1. Discuss the aspects of **Tableau Excellence.**

2. Invite student actors to incorporate the **dramatic coaching points** and recreate the Tableau so that it is theatrically more powerful.

3. Once they are ready, provide the same cues: *"Action – 2 – 3 - Freeze!"*

4. View (and perhaps photograph) the revised Tableau. Then call *"Relax."*

5. The second draft of the Tableau is consistently much stronger than the first.

6. Compliment the student actors on improved energy, expression, and levels.

7. **Teaching Tip:** If students are not able to maintain stillness and silence, it's fine to challenge them to try the Tableau again. If certain students remain unable to control their laughter and cooperate with the group, you may invite them to join you as audience members and respectfully watch the rest of the students create the Tableau. Allow them to re-join the student actors when they feel capable of cooperating.

Tableau Excellence

A Tableau involves a group of actors playing roles who position themselves to create a silent frozen picture that represents a significant moment in a story.

Actors…

…remain still or frozen.
The actors cooperate as members of an ensemble when the drama task requires stillness.

…remain silent.
The actors respond to signals (cues) requiring quiet focus.

…pose with energy.
The actors enhance character portrayals by posing with appropriate vitality and intensity.

…pose with expression.
The actors use facial expressions that communicate the thoughts and feelings of the characters.

…keep their concentration.
The actors focus intently on the drama task, remain in character, and control their laughter.

…pose at different levels.
The actors work with others to create interesting stage pictures that include actors posed in low, medium, and high positions.

…pose with an audience in mind.
The actors collaborate to ensure that each actor's pose and face (as appropriate) are visible to observers.

…choose poses that reflect the mood of the dramatized moment.
The actors enhance the dramatic experience or setting with appropriate poses and facial expressions.

Adapted from the book *A Dramatic Approach to Reading Comprehension* by Lenore Blank Kelner and Rosalind M. Flynn
www.RosalindFlynn.com

Reflect on the Whole Group Tableau

Refer back to the **Tableau Excellence chart** and ask students reflect on the effectiveness of their second Tableau. They can always recognize the big differences between the first one and the second one they created following incorporation of the **dramatic coaching points**. If the technology is available, let students see the digital images of their Tableau first and second drafts and comment on the changes.

Pose any or all of the following questions:

♦ *What were some differences between the first draft of your Tableau and the second draft?*

♦ *Look at the Tableau Excellence chart. What did we do well? What might we improve upon?*

♦ *As an actor in a Tableau, what do you need to work on?*

Repeat the Same Tableau with Half of the Group

Because the entire group created the initial Tableau, you (the teacher or leader) were likely the only one who got to see it. To give students the experience of 1.) presenting a Tableau for an audience, 2.) observing a Tableau, and 3.) improving the quality of a Tableau, lead them through the following next steps:

1. Explain the upcoming activity to students. *"To give you a chance to perform your Tableau for an audience and also to observe a Tableau, half of you will recreate the same Tableau we just did while half of you observe. Then we'll switch so that you will all get a chance to perform and observe."*

2. Identify the performance space—generally the front of the room you are in—which may require moving a few pieces of furniture to make a small amount of room.

3. Invite half of the group up to the performance space. (**Teaching Tip:** If you need to prompt participation, tell students to think of the day of the month on which they were born. Tell them that students born on even days will present the Tableau first while students born on odd days will observe. This generally results in "halving" the group.)

4. Identify a new focal point in the back of the room—in this case, the imagined alien space ship—so that all student actors share the same focus.

5. Explain to students that the actors in the performance space will strike and hold their poses on cue (*"Action-2-3-Freeze!"*). The observing students will function like stage directors who help actors improve their stage pictures—their Tableaux (plural of Tableau!).

6. **Teaching Tip:** The following warning is one that you may want to give repeatedly: *"Audience, if you like what you see, it's fine to laugh, but please—no comments. Comments make it difficult for the actors to keep their concentration and remain frozen in the Tableau."*

7. Once you feel that the student actors (and audience) are ready, cue them with *"Action – 2 – 3 - Freeze!"*

8. View the Tableau for about 10 seconds and then call *"Relax."*

9. Have the actors remain in the performance space. Ask the observers to consider the **Tableau Excellence Chart** and compliment the actors on what they did well.

10. Then ask the observers to offer suggestions to the actors for improving their Tableau. (Most common suggestions include: Changes in positions to get more variation in levels, changes in positions of arms, and adjustments of bodies and faces so that they are visible to the audience.)

11. Note: Each student actor has the final choice of whether to use an observer's recommendation. The actors are not required to follow directions they disagree with, but they are usually good about making the suggested adjustments.

12. Prepare students to recreate the same Tableau.

13. Again, remind the observers: *"Audience, if you like what you see, it's fine to laugh, but please—no comments. Comments make it difficult for the actors to keep their concentration and remain frozen in the Tableau."*

14. Once you feel that the student actors are ready to create the revised Tableau, cue them with *"Action – 2 – 3 - Freeze!"*

15. View the Tableau for about 10 seconds and then call *"Relax."*

16. Thank the first half of the student actors and ask them to take their seats. Invite the remaining half to come up to the performance space.

17. Repeat the same process (Steps 4 -16).

Reflect on the Half Group Tableaux

Refer back to the **Tableau Excellence chart** and ask students reflect on their experiences of viewing a Tableau and performing in a Tableau.

Pose any or all of the following questions:

- *How did viewing a Tableau before and after the changes increase your understanding of what makes an effective Tableau?*
- *What are the differences between creating a whole group Tableau with everyone in the room and creating a Tableau for an audience?*
- *What Tableau skills do you need to work on?*

More Group Tableau Possibilities

If you would like to give students additional practice—either as a whole group or in smaller groups—here are some ideas of circumstances and settings:

- Reporters and photographers who spot a big celebrity
- Fans—both happy and angry—at a sporting event
- Tourists looking at a famous site
- People watching fireworks

You may use the reproducible **Tableau Tasks** on the following pages to communicate Tableau goals to students when they work in small groups. You may fill in the blanks before handing them to students or you may have students complete the form.

The Purpose of the Process

This set of introductory Tableau activities prepares students to use this drama strategy with significant moments in the literature that they read and the historical episodes that they study. It provides them with a foundation for future productive use of Tableau in small groups. Strong theatre skills contribute to effective Tableaux.

Tableau Task

Your group will create a Tableau of _____
_____
_____

Book pages (if applicable): _____

Setting: _____

Characters: Actors:

_____   _____
_____   _____
_____   _____
_____   _____
_____   _____
_____   _____
_____   _____

Director: _____

1. Determine the details of the setting, characters, and event(s) in your scene.
2. Visualize and discuss the scene's event(s) and character poses.
3. Discuss the characters' possible thoughts and feelings.
4. Determine which student actors will play which characters.
5. If desired, choose one person as your group's director.
6. Plan and rehearse your Tableau. (As you make decisions, remember to keep in mind where your audience will be.)
7. Keep the components of the **Tableau Excellence** chart in mind as you work.
8. Rehearse your Tableau.
9. Present your Tableau for the whole group.

Effective Tableau Text

Look for:

- Action—scenes in which characters do something, interact with one another, move, react…
- Scenes in which characters react emotionally
- Incidents that are mentioned only briefly in a text
- Scenes that would make good book illustrations
- Scenes that would make interesting photographs
- Dream or nightmare scenes
- Scenes that occur in a character's imagination

Avoid:

- Descriptive text with little or no action
- Scenes that are too long or have too many different characters
- Scenes in which there is much dialogue, but little action
- Love scenes!
- Scenes that involve magic or special effects too difficult to depict
- Casting students as animals—unless the students can play the roles either as animals that exhibit human traits or with the necessary concentration and self-control. (Playing an animal can cause some students to use the opportunity to draw unnecessary attention to themselves and detract from the overall Tableau.)

Tableau Examples from Curriculum

Children's Literature

- *Mufaro's Beautiful Daughters* by John Steptoe.

    Characters: Manyara, boy, Nyasha, trees

    1. Manyara scolds the little boy.

    2. Nyasha gives the little boy some food.

    3. In the forest, Manyara passes trees who laugh at her. She laughs back at them.

- *The Day Jimmy's Boa Ate the Wash* by Trinka Hakes Noble

    Characters: School children, Jimmy, boa constrictor (if desired)

    A bunch of school children on a field trip to a farm throw eggs at each other. Jimmy drops his boa constrictor when he gets involved in the egg throwing.

- *The Araboolies of Liberty Street* by Sam Swope

    Characters: Araboolies, neighbors

    The Araboolie family makes a noisy arrival in a van. Their astonished neighbors watch in disbelief.

- *The Legend of the Bluebonnet* by Tommie DePaola

    Create Tableaux of these moments depicted by quotes from the text:

    Characters: The Comanche people

    1. "Great Spirits, the land is dying. Your people are dying, too!"

    2. "Tell us what we have done to anger you. End this drought. Save your people.

    3. "Tell us what we must do so you will send the rain that will bring back life."

- *Frindle* by Andrew Clements

    Characters: Nick, Mrs. Granger, students

    Nick drives his teacher crazy by inventing a new word for a pen.

♦ *Where the Wild Things Are* by Maurice Sendak

Characters: Max, wild things

1. Max is where the wild things are. The creatures roar, gnash their teeth, roll their eyes, and show their claws.
2. Max shouts, "Be still!" He stares into the eyes of the wild things. They are frightened and calmed.
3. The wild things call Max "The Most Wild Thing of All!"

♦ *Abel's Island* by William Steig

Characters: Abel, Amanda, friends

When Abel and Amanda take shelter from a big storm, Abel tries to get Amanda's scarf and gets sucked away.

♦ *Justin and the Best Biscuits in the World* by Mildred Pitts Walter

Characters: Justin, Hadiya, Evelyn, Momma

Justin's sister says he can't do a thing right and Momma grounds him because his room is a mess and he made a mess in the kitchen.

♦ *The BFG* by Roald Dahl

Characters: BFG, Sophia, Bonecrusher

When Bonecrusher smells "human" in BFG's cave, Sophia hides.

Young Adult Literature

♦ *Diary of a Young Girl* by Anne Frank

Characters: Anne Frank, Mr. and Mrs. Frank, Margot, Mr. and Mrs. Van Daan, Peter, Mr. Dussel

The people in hiding hold a Hanukkah celebration.

♦ *To Kill A Mockingbird* by Harper Lee

Characters: Tom Robinson, the whites, jury, witnesses, the blacks, Scout, Jem, Judge Taylor, Atticus

At Tom Robinson's trial in the Maycomb County courthouse, Atticus questions Robinson on the witness stand.

- *Sarah, Plain and Tall* by Patricia MacLachlan

  Characters: Papa, Sarah, Anna, Caleb

  Papa yells to Sarah, Anna, and Caleb—"A squall!" They see a huge, horribly black cloud moving across the fields toward them.

- *Little House on the Prairie* by Laura Ingalls Wilder

  Characters: Laura, Mary, Ma, two Indians

  Laura and Mary enter the log cabin and find two Indians with fierce expressions waiting while Ma cooks them cornbread.

- *The Outsiders* by S. E. Hinton

  Characters: Ponyboy, the Socs

  A group of Socs surrounds Ponyboy and "jump" him.

- *Shiloh* by Phyllis Reynolds Naylor

  Characters: Marty, Judd, Pa, Ma, Shiloh (Could be indicated by stuffed animal or a coat.)

  Judd comes to the Preston's house and discovers that Marty has been hiding his dog, Shiloh, from him and allowed Shiloh to get badly wounded.

- *The Adventures of Tom Sawyer* by Mark Twain

  1. Characters: Tom, Jim

  To get Jim to whitewash the fence, Tom tries to bribe him with a marble. (Chapter 2)

  Search for this text: *Say, Jim, I'll fetch the water if you'll whitewash some.*

  2. Characters: Tom, Ben

  Ben Rogers begs Tom to be allowed to whitewash the fence. (Chapter 2)

  Search for this text: *Does a boy get a chance to whitewash a fence every day?*

  3. Characters: Judge Thatcher, Mr. Walter, Librarian, teachers, pupils
  Members of the congregation react when Tom presents the tickets and wins the Bible. (Chapter 4)

  Search for this text: *And now at this moment, when hope was dead, Tom Sawyer came forward with nine yellow tickets, nine red tickets, and ten blue ones, and demanded a Bible.*

4. Characters: Tom, Huck

Tom and Huck think they hear dead people coming for them in the graveyard. (Chapter 9)

Search for this text: *And the two clung together with beating hearts.*

5. Characters: Tom, Aunt Polly, Sid, Mary, Joe Harper's mother

From under the bed, Tom listens to mournful talk about the missing boys. (Chapter 15)

Search for this text: *There sat Aunt Polly, Sid, Mary, and Joe Harper's mother, grouped together, talking.*

6. Characters: Tom, Joe, Huck, the minister, and the congregation

The minister, the boys' families, and the members of the congregation react when Tom, Joe, and Huck appear at their own funeral service. (Chapter 17)

Search for this text: *The villagers began to gather, loitering a moment in the vestibule to converse in whispers about the sad event.*

Shakespeare's Plays

♦ *Macbeth*

Characters: Macbeth, Banquo, three witches

Macbeth and Banquo listen to the prophesies of the three witches.

♦ *Julius Caesar*

Characters: Caesar, Brutus, Cassius, Casca, Decius Brutus, Metellus Cimber, Cinna, Onlookers

The conspirators assassinate Caesar. (Cassius, Casca, Brutus, and the other conspirators with knives raised; Caesar saying "Et tu Brute? Then fall, Caesar.")

♦ *King Lear*

Characters: Lear, Cordelia, Regan, Goneril

King Lear and his daughters react when Cordelia refuses to declare total love and devotion to her father alone.

See also—individual Shakespearean slide descriptions under Human Slide Shows that follow.

Historical Events

- **Christopher Columbus** and his crew on deck the moment that land is first sighted

- **Native Americans** on land the moment that they spot Columbus's ships

- A **Salem witchcraft trial**

- The signing of the **Declaration of Independence**

- **Rosa Parks** refusing to surrender her seat on the bus

- **Cherokees** on the **Trail of Tears**

- **Harriet Tubman** leading fugitives to stations on the **Underground Railroad**.

- Women marching for **suffrage**

Incorporating Dialogue into a Tableau

Tableau drama activities can be expanded by the creation and incorporation of **dialogue**. Once you have led students through the activities in **Introducing Tableau to Students,** you can enrich this drama experience by inviting students to deepen the inferences they make about what the characters in a Tableau are thinking and feeling.

On the cue of a touch of a shoulder or—as students become more experienced—a line delivered by another actor, the student actors speak their characters' thoughts aloud and increase the learning potential of this drama activity. Here's how:

Prepare the Student Actors

1. Tell the student actors that there is a way to add **lines of dialogue** to a Tableau.
2. Explain that, while they are holding their frozen Tableau positions, you will circulate among them and touch the shoulder of each individual. This is the actor's **cue**—a signal for the individual to speak aloud in role as his or her character.
3. The words that the student actors create could be the character's thoughts (called **"subtext"** by actors) or the words could be **lines of dialogue** (such as a playwright might write) if this Tableau were a scene from a play.
4. Use the same alien space ship sighting circumstance (or choose a different circumstance) and ask for volunteers willing to model this version of the Tableau while other students observe.
5. Give the students some "think time" to come up with a line or two of dialogue for the character that each will play. You may allow them to plan in pairs.
6. You may allow them to write their lines down, but if they do, ask them to memorize their written lines as best as they can for the Tableau presentation. (Writing the lines can be a great strategy, but the Tableau

is less dramatic if, when the actors are cued to speak, they read from a piece of paper.)

7. **Teaching Tip:** If necessary, remind the student actors to create appropriate dialogue—no profanity or bathroom language, no anachronisms, etc. Their words should enhance the intended mood of the Tableau and communicate some information about characters and circumstances.

Example: In the Tableau that depicts students sighting an alien space ship landing in their schoolyard, the lines of dialogue that student actors create might be like the following:

"I can't believe my eyes!"

"What? What? What is it?"

"Oh, no!"

"Let's get out of here!"

A Reminder about Depicting Violence and Weapons: I've learned that it's a good idea to remind students that in this Tableau (and in many others), our goal is to avoid incorporating words and actions of violence and the use of weapons. This goal has to do partly with the fact that our drama work is taking place in an educational setting. But, the more important purpose of this restriction is that we are working for more creative solutions to dramatic problems. Violence and weapons are not creative solutions.

Try to remember to communicate this to students before they create the Tableau and the dialogue. If you forget (as I sometimes do), add this to your goals for the second draft of the same Tableau.

However... If a Tableau depicts a scene of violence from a play (like the scene in which Claudius kills Hamlet's father), then, of course, that's an exception to the words of advice above.

Generate Dialogue with "Shoulder Touch"

1. Invite the Tableau actors to the performance space. Ask them to stand in **actor's neutral**—weight evenly balanced on both feet, hands by their sides, faces expressionless.

2. **Teaching Tip:** As mentioned previously, before you begin each Tableau presentation, remind the audience that they are welcome to laugh appropriately if they enjoy what they see and hear, but they are not to make comments. (Comments make it difficult for student actors to maintain their concentration and hold their frozen poses.)

3. Remind the student actors to pose with energy and expression, to concentrate, and to incorporate a variety of levels to create a strong Tableau. (Refer again to the Tableau Excellence chart.)

4. Encourage the student actors to speak loudly enough—to use effective **voice projection**—to **articulate**—speak clearly and not too quickly—and to use effective **vocal expression**.

5. Cue the student actors to take and hold their Tableau poses by saying, *"Action – 2 - 3 – Freeze!"*

6. While the student actors freeze silently in their Tableau poses, circulate among them, and cue them to deliver their dialogue by touching each student actor's shoulder.

7. Note: You may direct students to maintain their Tableau poses even as they speak or you may allow them to break their pose and move when they deliver their lines and then "re-freeze" in position afterwards.

8. Once every student actor has delivered a line, cue the end of the Tableau presentation by saying *"Relax."*

9. Note: I recommend letting students experience generating dialogue in a Tableau with Shoulder Touch before sharing the **Tableau Lines of Dialogue Excellence chart** with them. Once they have experienced it—either as actors or audience members—they have a stronger idea of how it works. Then you can focus on how to improve the work.

Tableau Lines of Dialogue Excellence

Share the **Tableau Lines of Dialogue Excellence chart** on the opposite page. Project it with a document camera or reproduce the list below on a chart or chalkboard.

> **Tableau Lines of Dialogue Excellence**
>
> Actors create lines that...
>
> ...<u>fit the characters</u> they are playing.
>
> ...<u>show an understanding</u> of the story or situation.
>
> ...communicate the <u>mood</u> of the story or situation.
>
> ...if instructed, use at least 1 <u>vocabulary word</u>.
>
> <u>Actors speak lines...</u>
>
> ...<u>loudly</u>.
>
> ...<u>clearly</u>.
>
> ...<u>with expression</u>.
>
> ...<u>with concentration</u>.
>
> ...<u>on cue</u>.

> **Note re: incorporating vocabulary words:** Ask students to disregard that element of the chart for now. Once they have practiced generating dialogue in Tableaux, you'll address that element.

Student Directors

If you think that using student directors for Tableaux (and Human Slide Shows, detailed in upcoming pages) would work for your students, you may certainly appoint one per scene or let each group choose one. The role of the director often suits students who would prefer not to perform. It's also beneficial because it helps to have a non-performer who can view each "stage picture" and offer ideas for adjustments in poses and positions to improve the presentation.

Tableau Lines of Dialogue Excellence

Actors enrich Tableau drama activities with the creation and delivery of dialogue. While in their frozen poses and on cue (a touch on the shoulder or a line delivered by another actor), the actors speak their characters' thoughts aloud.

Actors create lines that…

…fit the characters they are playing.

The actors invent lines that accurately communicate the thoughts and feelings of the characters.

…show an understanding of the story or situation.

The actors invent lines that accurately communicate information about the dramatic circumstance.

…communicate the mood of the story or situation.

The actors invent lines that reflect the appropriate tone and mood of the dramatic circumstance.

…if instructed, use at least one vocabulary word.

The actors' lines incorporate the specific vocabulary of the dramatic circumstance.

Actors speak lines…

…loudly. The actors project—speak with appropriate volume.

…clearly. The actors articulate. They pronounce words precisely and speak slowly enough to be understood.

…with expression. The actors' voices communicate the characters' personalities, moods, and emotions via tone of voice, emphasis, inflection, tempo, etc.

…with concentration. The actors focus intently on the drama task, remain in character, and control their laughter.

…on cue. The actors respond to signals—such as a touch on the shoulder or a line delivered by another actor.

Adapted from the book *A Dramatic Approach to Reading Comprehension* by Lenore Blank Kelner and Rosalind M. Flynn
www.RosalindFlynn.com

Reflect on the Tableau with Dialogue

1. Discuss the aspects of **Tableau Lines of Dialogue Excellence.**

2. With the students—both the actors and the audience—reflect on the effectiveness of the Tableau and dialogue.

   ♦ *How well did the lines of dialogue fit setting, characters, and circumstance?*

   ♦ *What were some strong lines of dialogue?*

   ♦ *What actors spoke with good expression and volume?*

   ♦ *How did adding dialogue change the Tableau experience?*

2. If the student actors had trouble maintaining their concentration or delivering their lines, you may want to conduct a second draft of the same Tableau.

3. Repeat the same Tableau with Dialogue with other groups of students, or have other groups create a different Tableau and practice delivering lines on the cue of a shoulder touch. Follow the same steps listed under **Generate Dialogue with "Shoulder Touch."**

Elevating the Dialogue in a Tableau

To deepen the drama work and connect it specifically to texts and curriculum, you can guide students to create stronger dialogue that incorporates vocabulary words and other subject-specific words into the lines they create within a Tableau. Here's how:

Prepare the Student Actors

1. Tell the student actors that, once again, while they are holding their frozen Tableau poses, you will circulate among them and touch the shoulder of each individual to signal the actor to speak a line of created dialogue.

2. This time, however, explain that the student actors must re-do or revise their dialogue by incorporating spelling/vocabulary words or words

that communicate appropriate elements of plot, character, theme, historical references, etc.

3. The dialogue, therefore, will be "elevated"—meaning that it incorporates specified words or phrases, and/or information that would increase an audience's understanding of the Tableau scene—words about characters, settings, previous actions, conflicts, etc.

4. Brainstorm with students a list of potential words or phrases for actors to incorporate into their lines of dialogue. (Note—if time is a factor, you may create this list and share it with students.)

Examples:

For a Tableau based on *Cinderella*, some scene-specific words that would strengthen lines of dialogue are: *stepsisters, stepmother, fairy godmother, prince, castle, palace, ball, glass slipper, coach, midnight, etc.*

For a Tableau based on *The Adventures of Tom Sawyer*: *Aunt Polly, Injun Joe, Becky, Hannibal, Mississippi River, schoolmaster, slate, raft, transfixed, pang, recollect.*

---

5. Display or project the list of words so that students "on stage" can see them. A chart for the sighting of the alien spaceship Tableau might look like this:

Alien Spaceship—Vocabulary words
Flying saucer
Aliens
Outer space
Galaxy
Milky Way
Extraterrestrial
E.T.
Mars
Martian
Earth
Planet
Spaceship
Moon
Solar system

6. Give the student actors some time to either revise a previous line ("Oh no," for example, could become, "Oh, no—an alien space ship!) or to create an entirely new line of dialogue.

7. Remind the student actors to create lines that use one or more of the words on the list in a meaningful way. The learning goal is to encourage greater and more specific language use. (Example: "Flying saucers!" is a line that would work, but "Do I see flying saucers landing in our schoolyard?" is even stronger.)

8. Draw students' attention once more to the **Excellence in Tableau Lines of Dialogue** chart.

Conduct the Tableau to Generate Elevated Dialogue

1. Once again, before you begin the Tableau presentation, remind the audience that they are welcome to laugh appropriately if they enjoy what they see and hear, but they are not to make comments.

2. Remind the student actors to pose with energy and expression, to concentrate, and to incorporate a variety of levels to create an interesting stage picture. (Posting the **Tableau Excellence** chart in clear sight provides a good reminder.)

3. Encourage the student actors to **project**—use effective vocal volume, to **articulate**—speak clearly and not too quickly, and to use effective **vocal expression**.

4. Cue the student actors to take and hold their Tableau poses: *"Action – 2 - 3 – Freeze!"*

5. While the student actors freeze silently in their Tableau poses, circulate among them and cue each to deliver a line of dialogue with a touch on the shoulder.

6. Once every student actor has delivered a line, cue the end of the Tableau presentation by saying, *"Relax."*

Reflect on the Tableau with Elevated Dialogue

1. With the students—both the actors and the audience—reflect on the effectiveness of the tableau and the incorporation of vocabulary words and scene-specific words.

   ♦ *How did adding vocabulary words change the lines of dialogue created?*

   ♦ *How did adding vocabulary words change the overall effect of the Tableau?*

2. Point out to students that the main way that playwrights communicate to audiences is through careful choices of words.

3. Guide the discussion, if necessary, to focus on how the intentional use of vocabulary words and/or words that communicate appropriate elements of plot, character, theme, or historical references strengthens lines of dialogue and therefore, the overall impact of the Tableau activity.

The Value of Vocabulary. Time and again, this dramatic approach to the creation and use of vocabulary words in Tableau presentations has motivated students to think more deeply and creatively, to return to the text and other curriculum materials to locate words and meanings, and to enjoy the challenge of the drama task. Elevating the dialogue in a Tableau is an authentic way to provide a purpose for using and speaking the meaningful words connected to a text or an area of study.

Allow Student Actors to Cue One Another

If you feel that your students have become adept at Tableau work, you can remove yourself from the presentation and eliminate the need for the "Shoulder Touch." Doing so will give students greater ownership of the Tableau they create and deepen the connection to the work that stage actors do. Here's how:

1. Tell students that they will create a Tableau with Lines of Dialogue, but that they will now need to work and plan together so that they cue one another instead of waiting for the Shoulder Touch.

2. Explain that in their rehearsal, they will need to share their lines of dialogue with one another and then determine the order in which they will deliver the lines.

3. Once the order is determined, they will need to decide who speaks first. The second student actor to deliver a line must know a.) who the first speaker is and b.) the gist of the line that will be delivered.

4. The third actor's cue is the end of the second actor's line…and so forth.

5. When the group is ready to perform, cue the student actors to take and hold their Tableau poses: *"Action – 2 - 3 – Freeze!"*

6. View the Tableau with Dialogue.

7. Once every student actor has delivered a line, cue the end of the Tableau presentation by saying *"Relax."*

Tableau with Dialogue Task

Your group will create a Tableau of _____

_____

_____

Book pages (if applicable): _____

Setting: _____

Characters: Actors:

_____   _____
_____   _____
_____   _____
_____   _____
_____   _____
_____   _____
_____   _____
_____   _____

Director: _____

1. Determine the details of the setting, characters, and event(s) in your scene.

2. Visualize and discuss the scene's event(s) and character poses.

3. Discuss the characters' possible thoughts and feelings.

4. Determine which student actors will play which characters.

5. Choose one person as your group's director.

6. Create lines of dialogue to speak aloud during the presentation of your tableau. (Your director will cue the spoken dialogue with "Shoulder Touch.")

7. Plan and rehearse your Tableau and lines of dialogue. (As you make decisions, remember to keep in mind where your audience will be.)

8. Keep the components of the **Tableau Excellence** and **Tableau Lines of Dialogue Excellence** charts in mind as you work.

9. Present your Tableau for the whole group.

Reflect on Student Actors Cueing One Another

With the students—both the actors and the audience—reflect on the effectiveness of this change in the Tableau presentation.

♦ *What was challenging about rehearsing and presenting this different way of delivering the Tableau with Dialogue?*

♦ *What was the overall effect of the Tableau when the "Shoulder Touch" was not used as the cue?*

Closing Comment

Once your students have learned to incorporate dialogue into a Tableau, they can use this drama strategy repeatedly to strengthen their understandings of the literature and history that they read. The more they do Tableau work, the more skilled they become and the more quickly they can move from the page to the stage.

Human Slide Shows

Human Slide Shows are series of Tableaux—several frozen pictures presented in chronological order to show what happened first, second, third, etc. in a sequence. Human Slide Shows are also called "Freeze-Frames" or simply "Slide Shows." To create the frozen, silent, concentrated poses, students must think like actors and directors who read to understand events and make artistic choices about how to stage the action so that an audience understands or infers what happens. Participation in Human Slide Shows works best when students have experienced the Tableau drama strategy.

Reinforcing Reading Comprehension Skills

Engaging in Human Slide Shows requires students to read and re-read a text and use these reading comprehension skills:

Determining Importance: Which four or five moments in the selected scene from the text or event are the best choices to be depicted as slides?

Developing Sensory Images: What are the sights, sounds, smells, tastes, and textures described in the text and how can student actors use their bodies and faces to communicate those sensory images?

Inferring: What is really going on in the scene? The characters may say one thing, but their thoughts, intentions, tactics, and expressions may be remarkably different from what they say. How can the student actors playing characters use silent, still poses to communicate the inferences they make about the text?

Practicing Theatre Skills

Human Slide Show rehearsals and performances also involve students in the thinking and the choices involved in the staging of a play:

Blocking: This is a term for the basic stage movements and positions of the actors playing characters during the presentation of the play.

Character motivations: What are the reasons for a character's behavior? Why does he or she do or say something?

Subtext: A character's thinking—the real reason why he or she does something and the true meaning beneath spoken words.

Introducing Human Slide Shows to Students

1. Explain to students that the drama strategy Human Slide Shows provides a way to show what happened in a sequence of events, one Tableau at a time.

2. Display a poster on which a Human Slide Show sequence is numbered and described. I find it effective to **model the Human Slide Show** with a portion of a familiar story that involves only two characters. This sequence from *Snow White* works well:

    1. The Evil Queen offers Snow White a poisoned apple.
    2. Snow White takes a bite.
    3. Snow White chokes.
    4. Snow White "dies."

    (Note: Encourage males to volunteer to play these characters. Assure them that an "all male cast" is perfectly fine and fun.)

3. Solicit two student actors to play the character roles and to model the drama strategy while the remaining students observe.

4. Work with the student actors and the observers to plan out the frozen poses for each Tableau in the Human Slide Show sequence.

5. Practice each pose in the sequence. Invite the observers to make suggestions to the student actors. (But avoid taking too many suggestions!) If the student actors like a suggestion, they can incorporate it into their pose. (Let each individual student actor choose whether to use suggestions.)

6. Explain that to create the slide show, the first cue for the actors and audience will be you saying ***"Blackout."*** This cue signals audience members to close their eyes while the student actors assume the Tableau pose.

7. Explain that the second cue for the actors and audience is ***"Lights up."*** This cue signals the audience members to open their eyes and view the student actors in the frozen "slide" until you call ***"Blackout"*** and so forth until each frame has been viewed in this fashion.

8. Tell everyone that after the final slide has been viewed, you will call *"Blackout"* once more. That's the cue for the actors to prepare to take a bow. They will un-freeze and be ready to bow and receive audience appreciation when you say *"Lights up."*

Conduct the Model Human Slide Show

1. Ask an audience member to hold the sequence-of-events chart so that the student actors can see it.

2. Ask the student actors to stand in **"actor's neutral"**—Actors stand with their weight evenly balanced on both feet, hands by their sides, faces expressionless.

3. Ascertain that both audience members and student actors are ready.

4. **Teaching Tip Reminder:** The following warning is one that you may want to give/repeat: *"Audience, remember that if you like what you see, it's fine to laugh, but please—no comments. Comments make it difficult for the actors to keep their concentration and remain frozen."*

5. Give the cue *"Blackout"* to signal audience members to close their eyes while the student actors assume the first pose in the slide.

6. During the Blackout, you may choose to narrate—read the slide description aloud so that everyone knows what the upcoming slide is. *("The Evil Queen Offers Snow White a poisoned apple.")* You may prefer to keep this a silent activity. Either choice works.

7. When you see that the student actors are ready, give the cue *"Lights up"* to signal audience members to open their eyes while the student actors remain frozen in the first slide pose.

8. Pause to view the slide (~6 to 10 seconds). Then give the *"Blackout"* cue.

9. If you choose, read the next slide description aloud while the audience's eyes are closed. *("Snow White takes a bite.")*

10. When the student actors are frozen in the next pose, give the *"Lights up"* cue.

11. Continue in this fashion until the final "slide"—the student actors' bow.

Reflect on the Model Human Slide Show

1. With the students—both the actors and the audience—reflect on the effectiveness of the model Human Slide Show.

    ♦ *Audience—How effective was the Human Slide Show for you? What contributed to making it work?*

    ♦ *Actors—What was challenging about performing the Human Slide Show?*

2. Now that the students know what a Human Slide Show is, discuss and share the criteria for excellence in this drama strategy.

Human Slide Shows Excellence

Share the **Human Slide Shows Excellence** chart on the opposite page. Project it using a document camera or reproduce the list below on a chart or chalkboard.

Human Slide Shows Excellence

Actors...

...remain <u>still</u> when cued.

...remain <u>silent</u> when cued.

...pose with <u>energy</u>.

...pose with <u>expression</u>.

...maintain <u>concentration</u>.

...pose at different <u>levels</u>.

...pose with an <u>audience</u> in mind.

...<u>alter</u> poses from one slide to the next.

...change poses <u>quickly</u> and <u>quietly</u>.

Human Slide Shows Excellence

Human Slide Shows are a series of Tableaux—frozen pictures made by actors—presented in chronological order—that show what happens first, second, third, etc., in a sequence of events.

Actors...

...remain still when cued.

The cue "Blackout" signals the audience to close their eyes and the actors to assume and hold their Tableau/slide poses. The cue "Lights up" signals audience members to open their eyes and observe the "slide." Actors remain perfectly still or frozen from "Lights up" until the next "Blackout" cue. During the "Blackout," actors create the next Tableau in the slide show.

...remain silent when cued.

The actors respond to signals (cues) requiring quiet focus.

...pose with energy.

The actors enhance character portrayals by posing with appropriate vitality and intensity.

...pose with expression.

The actors use facial expressions that communicate the thoughts and feelings of the characters and the appropriate tone and mood of the slide sequence.

...maintain concentration.

The actors focus intently on the drama task, remain in character, and control their laughter.

...pose at different levels.

The actors work with others to create interesting stage pictures that include actors posed in low, medium, and high positions.

...pose with an audience in mind.

The actors collaborate to ensure that each actor's pose and face (as appropriate) are visible to observers.

...alter poses from one slide to the next.

The actors change body positions and facial expressions to show a progression of the scene's action.

...change poses quickly and quietly.

The actors execute the slide transitions with no distracting noise or delays.

Adapted from the book *A Dramatic Approach to Reading Comprehension* by Lenore Blank Kelner and Rosalind M. Flynn
www.RosalindFlynn.com

Here's the same list with each factor elaborated on for clarity:

Human Slide Shows Excellence

Actors...

- remain **still** when cued.

  The cue "Blackout," signals the student actors to assume and hold their poses. The cue "Lights up" signals audience members to open their eyes and observe the slide. Student actors who remain perfectly still from each "Lights up" until each "Blackout" cue preserve the illusion of a slide show.

- remain **silent** when cued.

  The Human Slide Show does not incorporate dialogue, so the job of the student actors is to hold quiet and frozen poses.

- pose with **energy.**

  Because each slide is meant to convey an important moment in the story, student actors who strike strong poses contribute to the overall positive effect of the Human Slide Show.

- pose with **expression.**

  The face of an actor can communicate an immense amount of information about the circumstances and the character portrayed. Accuracy in chosen facial expressions also indicates how well students understand the text or event that they depict as a Human Slide Show.

- maintain **concentration.**

  A strong Human Slide Show will be far less effective if the student actors are shaking with laughter (even silent laughter), so do emphasize the importance of concentration. Concentration will also help student actors present the slides.

- ...pose at different **levels.**

  To keep the Human Slide Show visually compelling (as in Tableau work), actors pose in variety of levels:
    - low to the ground (stooping, kneeling, lying)
    - medium level (bending, leaning, sitting)
    - high level (standing, reaching, stretching)

- pose with an **audience** in mind.

  Because this drama strategy is meant to inform audience members as well as student actors about the characters and events described in a text, it's important for the actors to position themselves so that their poses and faces can be seen by observers.

- **alter poses** from one slide to the next.

  The most compelling Human Slide Shows are those that offer an audience a distinctly different frozen picture each time they open their eyes. This aspect of excellence requires the student actors to explore alternative poses for their characters, even when it seems like a character does not change much from slide to slide.

- change poses **quickly** and **quietly.**

  During the "Blackout" portions of the Human Slide Show presentation, it's important for actors to move quietly— to avoid stomping footsteps, whispering, laughing, loud bangs of furniture serving as set pieces, etc. And it's best not to leave an audience in the dark for too long— especially if closed eyes create "the dark." (Noise and extended time prompts audience members to peek!) Also, the slides should, of course, be presented in the correct order!

You may use the reproducible **Human Slide Show Tasks** on the upcoming pages to communicate Human Slide Show goals to students when they work in small groups. You may fill in the blanks before handing them to students or you may have students complete the form.

A Snow White Human Slide Show

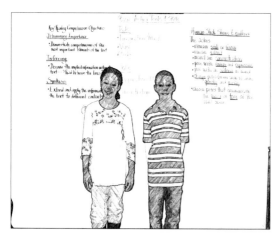

Actor's Neutral

3. Snow White chokes.

1. The Evil Queen offers Snow White an
   apple.

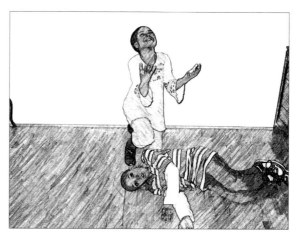

4. Snow White "dies."

2. Snow White takes a bite.

5. The actors take a bow.

Human Slide Show Task

Your group will create a Human Slide Show of _____
_____
_____

Book pages (if applicable): _____

Setting: _____

Characters: Actors:

_____   _____
_____   _____
_____   _____
_____   _____
_____   _____

Director: _____

1. Determine the details of the setting, characters, and events in your scene.
2. Brainstorm possible events or moments to depict as slides.
3. Determine the four or five most important moments to depict as slides.
4. Describe each slide (below and on the back of this page) in a simple sentence or two:

_____

_____

_____

_____

_____

_____

_____

5. Discuss the characters' possible thoughts, feelings, and poses.
6. Determine which student actors will play which characters.
7. Choose one person as your group's director.
8. Plan and rehearse your Human Slide Show.
9. Remember the components of **Human Slide Shows Excellence**.
10. Present your Human Slide Show for the whole group.

Human Slide Show Task

Your group will create the following Human Slide Show:

_____
_____
_____
_____
_____
_____
_____
_____
_____
_____
_____
_____
_____
_____
_____
_____
_____

Book pages (if applicable): _____

Setting: _____

Characters: Actors:

_____   _____
_____   _____
_____   _____
_____   _____
_____   _____

Director: _____

1. Determine the details of the setting, characters, and events in your scene.
2. Discuss the characters' possible thoughts, feelings, and poses.
3. Determine which student actors will play which characters.
4. Choose one person as your group's director.
5. Plan and rehearse your Human Slide Show.
6. Keep the components of the **Human Slide Shows Excellence** in mind.
7. Present your Human Slide Show for the whole group.

Presenting the Small Group Human Slide Shows

1. Invite the student actors and their director to the performance space.

2. Ask the student actors to stand in **"Actor's Neutral"**—Actors stand with their weight evenly balanced on both feet, hands by their sides, faces expressionless.

3. Ascertain that both audience members and student actors are ready.

4. **Teaching Tip Reminder:** The following warning (as mentioned earlier) is one that you may want to give/repeat: *"Audience, remember that if you like what you see, it's fine to laugh, but please—no comments. Comments make it difficult for the actors to keep their concentration and remain frozen."*

5. Give the cue *"Blackout"* to signal audience members to close their eyes while the student actors assume the first pose in the slide. *(Note: You may allow the student director to give this cue, but it can be complicated to give the "Blackout" cue, read the slide description, and give the "Lights Up" cue, so I often give these cues and have the director read the slide description.)*

6. Remember that during the Blackout, you or the student director may narrate—read the slide description aloud so that everyone knows what the upcoming slide is *("The Evil Queen Offers Snow White a poisoned apple.")* or you may keep this transition silent. Either choice works.

7. When the student actors are ready, the cue *"Lights up"* signals audience members to open their eyes while the student actors remain frozen in the first slide pose.

8. Pause to view the slide (~6 to 10 seconds) and hear the lines of dialogue. Then give the *"Blackout"* cue.

9. If desired, read the next slide description aloud while the audience's eyes are closed. *("Snow White takes a bite.")*

10. When the student actors are frozen in the next pose, give the *"Lights up"* cue.

11. Continue in this fashion until the final "slide"—the student actors' bow.

Reflecting on Human Slide Shows

With the students—both the actors and the audience—reflect on the effectiveness of the model Human Slide Show.

Audience—How effective was the Human Slide Show for you? What contributed to making it work?

Actors—What was challenging about performing the Human Slide Show?

Audience—Do you have any recommendations for strengthening the Human Slide Show?

Adding Dialogue to a Human Slide Show

Students often ask if they can add dialogue to their Human Slide Shows. The answer is yes. My feeling is that it's best—aesthetically speaking—to eliminate the cue of the "Shoulder Touch," and—as previously described in **Allow Student Actors to Cue One Another via Dialogue**—require student actors to cue themselves.

Adding multiple lines of dialogue per student actor to a Human Slide Show further deepens the connection to the work that stage actors do. Here's how:

1. Tell students that they will add lines of dialogue to their Human Slide Show.

2. They will work together so that they cue one another in each slide.

3. Explain that in their rehearsal of each slide, they will need to plan and share their lines of dialogue and determine the order in which they will deliver the lines.

4. For <u>each</u> <u>slide</u>, they will need to decide who speaks first. The second student actor to deliver a line must know a.) who the first speaker is and b.) the gist of the line that will be delivered.

5. The third actor's cue is the end of the second actor's line…and so forth.

6. To present the Human Slide Show, you or the student director will give the cue *"Blackout"* to signal audience members to close their eyes while the student actors assume the first pose in the slide.

7. During the Blackout, you (or the student director) may choose to narrate—read the slide description aloud so that everyone knows what the upcoming slide is. *("Red Riding Hood meets up with the Big Bad Wolf.")* You may prefer to keep this a silent activity. Either choice works.

8. When you (or the student director) see that the student actors are ready/frozen in position, give the cue, ***"Lights up"*** to signal audience members to open their eyes while the student actors remain frozen in the first slide pose.

9. Note: You may allow the student actors to move when they speak and then resume their poses or you may require them to remain frozen with only their mouths (of course) moving. Either option works.

10. Pause to view the slide and allow the student actors to deliver their lines of dialogue. Then give the ***"Blackout"*** cue.

11. Continue in this fashion until the final "slide"—the student actors' bow.

Slide Descriptions

Please note that the sentences that describe each slide are brief—very brief. This is intentional. The sequence-of-events list is meant to cue the actors. Just as professional actors do to prepare to portray characters and events, student actors need to make inferences, examine the text for details, discuss alternatives, and familiarize themselves with the material. Then they must rehearse to use their faces, bodies, and (sometimes) voices to communicate their understandings.

See examples of brief slide descriptions on the following pages.

Number of Slides per Human Slide Show

For beginners to this drama strategy and for younger students, I recommend a limit of four slides. The time required for research, discussion, planning, and rehearsal is reasonable with four slides. Give students practice with four slides and when they are adept at Human Slide Shows, they will be able to handle the preparation needed for more than four.

Human Slide Show Examples from Curriculum

Children's Literature

The Legend of the Bluebonnet by Tommie DePaola

    Characters: The People and She-Who-Is-Alone

    1. For three days, the dancers dance to the sound of the drums.

    2. The People called Comanche watch and wait for the rain.

    3. She-Who-Is-Alone speaks to her doll.

    4. The People hear that the shaman is returning.

The Legend of the Bluebonnet by Tommie DePaola

    Characters: The People, She-Who-Is-Alone, and the Shaman

    1. The People gather to hear the shaman.

    2. The shaman tells that the Great Spirits say the People have been selfish.

    3 The shaman tells them they must make sacrifices to end the drought.

    4. The People sing a song of thanks to the Great Spirits.

Nessa's Fish by Nancy Luenn

    Characters: Nessa, Grandmother

    1. Nessa and her grandmother fish in the stony lake.

    2. They catch more fish than they can carry home.

    3. Nessa and her grandmother stack up the fish.

    4. Then they fall asleep.

Heckedy Peg by Audrey Wood

    Characters: Brothers, sisters, the witch

    1. The brothers and sisters are happily playing when a witch taps on their window.

    2. The witch asks the children to let her in and to give her a light for her pipe. The children refuse.

    3. The witch promises them a sack of gold. They bring her burning sticks of straw from the fire.

    4. The witch casts a spell on the children and turns them into various items of food.

The Town Mouse and the Country Mouse by Aesop

Characters: Country Mouse, Town Mouse, two dogs

1. The Country Mouse is amazed by the food on the table.
2. The two mice begin to nibble.
3. Two dogs come bounding into the dining room.
4. The mice scamper back into the hole.
5. The Country Mouse says good-bye to his cousin the Town Mouse.

Young Adult Literature

The Watsons Go To Birmingham, 1963 by Christopher Paul Curtis

Characters: Kenny, Byron, Dad, Momma, Joetta

1. Kenny finds Byron with his lips frozen to the window of the car.
2. The family rushes outside to see what has happened to Byron.
3. Dad fights laughter as Mom tries to figure out how to pry Byron loose.
4. Kenny pours hot water on Byron.
5. Mom snatches Byron off the car.

Characters: Byron, Kenny

1. Byron offers his "free" cookies to Kenny.
2. Byron and Kenny notice the dove on the telephone wire.
3. Byron throws cookies at the bird.
4. Byron hits the bird.
5. Byron realizes that the bird is dead.

The Pearl by John Steinbeck

Characters: Juana, Kino

1. Juana begins to throw the pearl back into the sea.
2. Kino grabs Juana's arm.
3. Kino strikes Juana.
4. Juana falls among the boulders.

The Outsiders by S.E. Hinton

Characters: Ponyboy, Socs, Greasers, Darry

1. The Socs approach Ponyboy.

2. The Socs jump Ponyboy, pulling him to the ground.

3. Ponyboy screams.

4. The greasers chase the Socs away while Darry helps Ponyboy to his feet.

From the Mixed-up Files of Mrs. Basil E. Frankweiler by E.L. Konigsburg

Characters: Jamie, Claudia

1. Jamie spots a candy bar on the ground.

2. He picks it up. Claudia warns him not to eat it because it could contain drugs.

3. He takes a bite while Claudia looks at him in disgust.

4. Jamie pretends to pass out. Claudia stands stunned and ready to scream for help.

5. Jamie opens his eyes and smiles.

Bridge to Terabithia by Katherine Patterson

Characters: Leslie, Jess, racers, school children

1. The recess race begins.

2. Jess is in the lead. The crowd of kids cheers.

3. Leslie catches up with Jess.

4. She crosses the finish line 3 feet ahead of Jess.

5. She turns and smiles at him as he walks away. The other students are stunned.

The Sign of the Beaver by Elizabeth Speare

Characters: Matt, two Indians

1. Up in the tree, Matt is attacked by a swarm of bees.

2. He dives in to a pond.

3. He tries to swim, but his feet are tangled in weeds and he loses consciousness.

4. An Indian lifts Matt out of the water.

5. He awakes on dry ground to find two Indians bending over him.

Tuck Everlasting by Natalie Babbitt

Characters: Mae, Miles, Jesse, Tuck, Winnie, and the man in the yellow suit.

1. The man in the yellow suit confronts the Tucks and Winnie.

2. The man begins to drag Winnie away.

3. Mae grabs a shotgun, holds it like a club, and tells him to stop. The man refuses.

4. Mae swings the shotgun and smashes the man in the back of the skull.

5. The man drops to the ground with his eyes wide open.

Roll of Thunder, Hear My Cry by Mildred D. Taylor

Characters: Cassie, Stacey, Christopher-John, Little Man, and T.J.

1. Stacey spots the white kids' school bus and shouts, "Quick! Off the road!"

2. Everyone but Little Man scrambles up the steep bank. "But I'll get my clothes dirty!" protests Little Man as he keeps walking.

3. The bus sprays dirt and dust all over Little Man.

4. Little Man shakes a fist at the bus.

The Indian in the Cupboard by Lynne Reid Banks

Characters: Omri, Indian

1. Omri sees the Indian crouched in the cupboard

2. When Omri peers more closely, the Indian leaps to his feet and reaches for his knife.

3. Omri reaches to touch the Indian who leaps, shouts, and raises his knife.

4. The Indian stabs Omri's finger.

5. Omri puts his finger in his mouth.

The Adventures of Tom Sawyer by Mark Twain

Characters: Minister, members of the congregation, Tom, Joe, Huck

1. As the minister gives the funeral sermon, members of the congregation mourn.

2. Tom, Joe, and Huck appear at the back of the church.

3. The boys come marching up the aisle. The families are shocked and overjoyed.

4. Everyone sings a hymn of praise.

A Separate Peace by John Knowles

Characters: Phineas, Gene

1. At the base of the tree, Phineas proposes that he and Gene jump together from the branch into the water.

2. Phineas climbs the tree and beckons to Gene.

3. Gene holds the trunk, takes a step toward Phineas, bends his knees, and jounces the limb.

4. Phineas loses his balance and looks at Gene.

5. Phineas tumbles and falls.

Shakespeare's Plays

Students who read Shakespeare are often discouraged because the heightened language can make it difficult to understand the dialogue and near to impossible to visualize the action of the play. Engaging students in planning, rehearsing, and presenting Human Slide Shows of key scenes can dramatically increase their interest in the plays and their comprehension of the text.

Julius Caesar (Act II, Scene 2) Calpurnia tries to prevent Caesar from leaving.

Characters: Caesar, Calpurnia

1. In her sleep, Calpurnia cries out, predicting Caesar's murder.

2. Calpurnia tells Caesar that he is not to leave his house today.

3. Caesar declares that he will leave the house.

4. Calpurnia tries to convince him by sharing her fears of frightening and evil omens.

5. Caesar declares that he will still go forth.

Julius Caesar (Act III, Scene 1): The conspirators assassinate Caesar.

Characters: Caesar, Brutus, Cassius, Casca, Decius Brutus, Metellus Cimber, Cinna, Onlookers

1. Caesar and his followers enter the Capitol.

2. Metellus Cimber begs Caesar to end his brother's banishment. Caesar refuses.

3. The conspirators prepare to stab Caesar.

4. The conspirators stab Caesar.

5. Caesar says, "Et tu Brute? Then fall, Caesar!"

6. Caesar dies and the conspirators shout triumphantly to the onlookers.

Julius Caesar (Act III, Scene 2): Brutus permits Antony to speak to the crowd.

Characters: Brutus, Antony, The people of Rome

1. Brutus claims that he loves Rome and freedom more than he loved Caesar.

2. The crowd of Roman hails Brutus as their respected leader.

3. Brutus convinces the crowd to listen to Antony's speech.

4. Antony begins speaking and seems to reflect anti-Caesar sentiments.

5. Antony praises Brutus, but speaks of Caesar's virtues. The crowd becomes uncertain.

The Tempest (Act II, Scene 1)

Characters: Alonso, Gonzalo, Antonio, Sebastian, Ariel

1. While Alonso and Gonzalo sleep, Antonio works to persuade Sebastian to murder his brother so that Sebastian can inherit Alonso's crown.

2. While Antonio and Sebastian step aside to plan the murder, Ariel sings into Gonzalo's ear.

3. Antonio and Sebastian raise their swords above the sleeping men.

4. Gonzalo awakes and then wakes Alonso.

5. They question Antonio and Sebastian who make an excuse. Ariel leaves to inform Prospero.

King Lear (Act I, Scene 1)

Characters: Lear, Goneril, Regan, Cordelia

1. King Lear declares that he will divide his kingdom among his three daughters—Goneril, Regan, and Cordelia.

2. Lear challenges each daughter to express her love for him.

3. Goneril expresses limitless love.

4. Regan declares her father's love to be her greatest joy.

5. Cordelia states only that she loves her father as a daughter should—no more nor less.

6. King Lear disowns Cordelia.

A Midsummer Night's Dream (Act II, Scene 2)

Characters: Fairies, Titania, Oberon, Lysander, Hermia, Puck, Helena, Demetrius

1. Titania's fairies sing her to sleep.

2. Oberon squeezes juice from the magic flower onto Titania's eyelids.

3. Lysander and Hermia enter.

4. Lysander and Hermia sleep. Puck puts the flower's juice on Lysander's eyes.

5. Helena chases Demetrius.

6. Demetrius escapes. Helena wakes Lysander who immediately falls in love with her.

Romeo and Juliet (Act III, Scene 1)

Characters: Romeo, Benvolio, Mercutio, Tybalt, citizens

1. Romeo finds Benvolio and Mercutio arguing with Tybalt.

2. Tybalt tries to pick a fight with Romeo, but Romeo refuses to quarrel.

3. Mercutio, angered because Romeo refuses to fight, challenges Tybalt.

4. When Romeo and Benvolio intervene, Mercutio is fatally wounded.

5. Grief-stricken and angry over the death of his best friend, Romeo slays Tybalt.

6. Romeo flees as angry citizens gather.

Macbeth (Act I, Scene 7)

Characters: Macbeth, Lady Macbeth

1. Macbeth has second thoughts about the murder. Lady Macbeth questions him.

2. Macbeth tells her he will not proceed.

3. Lady Macbeth accuses him of cowardly behavior. She claims that she could be capable of murder.

4. Macbeth wonders what "if we should fail." Lady Macbeth protests: "Screw your courage to the sticking place!"

Macbeth (Act III, Scene 4)

Characters: Lady Macbeth, Ross, Lennox, lords, ladies, attendants, Banquo's Ghost

1. Lady Macbeth, Ross, Lennox, lords, and attendants sit at a banquet table. The First Murderer informs Macbeth of Banquo's death and Fleance's escape.

2. The First Murderer leaves. Lady Macbeth bids Macbeth to welcome his guests.

3. Banquo's Ghost takes Macbeth's seat at the table. Macbeth reacts strangely. Lady Macbeth tries to cover for him and calm the guests.

4. Lady Macbeth scolds Macbeth for his fearful behavior. The Ghost leaves.

5. Macbeth regains his composure and proposes a toast to Banquo and his guests.

Hamlet (Act V, Scene 2) The deaths at the end of the play

    Characters: Hamlet, Laertes, Claudius, Gertrude, Horatio

1. Hamlet and Laertes begin their sword fight.
2. Hamlet declines Claudius's offer of the poisoned cup.
3. Gertrude drinks from the poisoned cup. Laertes wounds Hamlet.
4. Their sword fight continues and they end up exchanging swords.
5. Gertrude dies. Hamlet wounds Laertes.
6. Hamlet then wounds Claudius with the sword and forces him to drink from the poisoned cup. Laertes dies.
7. Hamlet convinces Horatio not to commit suicide.
8. Hamlet dies.

Dramatic Literature

A Streetcar Named Desire **by Tennessee Williams**

    Characters: Stanley, Mitch, Stella

    Setting: The exterior of the Kowalski home

1. Stanley bellows up to Stella.
2. Stella appears and greets the men.
3. Stanley heaves a package of meat at Stella.
4. Stella catches it.
5. Stanley and Mitch leave. Stella follows.

    Characters: Blanche, Eunice, Colored Woman

    Setting: The exterior of the Kowalski home

1. Blanche enters and looks at her surroundings.
2. Eunice greets Blanche.
3. Blanche is surprised to learn that her sister lives in this place.
4. The Colored Woman leaves to get Stella.
5. Eunice takes Blanche into Stella's flat.

Character: Blanche

Setting: The interior of the Kowalski home

1. Blanche sits and looks around her at her sister's home.
2. Blanche notices a whiskey bottle.
3. Blanche pours herself a drink.
4. Blanche tosses the whiskey down her throat.
5. Blanche replaces the bottle and washes her glass.
6. Blanche returns to her seat.

Characters: Blanche, Stella

Setting: The interior of the Kowalski home

1. Stella calls out to Blanche.
2. Blanche and Stella stare at one another.
3. Blanche calls out to Stella.
4. Blanche and Stella embrace.
5. Blanche tells Stella to turn off the overhead light.
6. Blanche comments on Stella's home.

Characters: Blanche, Stella

Setting: The interior of the Kowalski home

1. Blanche looks around the house for some liquor.
2. Blanche finds the bottle and attempts to open it.
3. Stella sits Blanche down.
4. Stella looks for some soda.
5. Blanche asks where Stanley is.
6. Blanche refuses the soda and invites Stella to sit down and talk.

Characters: Blanche, Stella

Setting: The interior of the Kowalski home

1. Blanche gives a dramatic and accusatory explanation of the loss of Belle Reve, the family home.
2. Stella tells Blanche to stop.
3. Stella starts to leave and Blanche asks if Stella is crying.
4. Blanche asks for forgiveness.
5. Stella and Blanche hear the sound of men's voices.

Characters: Blanche, Stanley

Setting: The interior of the Kowalski Home

1. Stanley enters, sees Blanche, and stares at her.
2. Blanche introduces herself.
3. Stanley examines the whiskey bottle.
4. Stanley offers Blanche a shot of liquor; she refuses.
5. Stanley complains of the heat and begins to remove his shirt.
6. Stanley asks Blanche if she was once married and Blanche feels sick.

The Crucible by Arthur Miller

Characters: Betty, Abigail, Mercy, Mary

1. At the bedside of the sleeping Betty Parris, Abigail warns Mercy and Mary to remain silent about their involvement in a witchcraft-related ritual.
2. Betty awakens and becomes hysterical.
3. Betty tries to "fly" out the window by her bed. The girls stop her.
4. Abigail threatens harm to all three of them if they speak about their activities.

Historical Events

Immigrants to America

Characters: Immigrants

1. Cold, hungry, and tired immigrants to America huddle on the deck of a ship.

2. One immigrant spots the Statue of Liberty.

3. All the immigrants strain to see the Statue.

4. Together with their family and friends, or separately, the immigrants rejoice.

The Boston Massacre

Characters: Colonists, Redcoats

1. British soldiers ("Redcoats") stand guard on a cold, snowy day in Boston.

2. Colonists approach and taunt the soldiers.

3. Colonists throw rocks and snowballs at the Redcoats.

4. The Redcoats fire their guns into the crowd of unarmed colonists.

5. Five colonists die.

The Boston Tea Party

Characters: Colonists

1. Colonists disguise themselves as Indians.

2. Colonists sneak aboard the ship.

3. Colonists throw crates of tea overboard.

4. Colonists rejoice!

Lincoln's Assassination

Characters: Lincoln, Mrs. Lincoln, audience members, Booth

1. President Lincoln, his wife, and others watch a play.

2. Booth approaches.

3. Booth shoots Lincoln.

4. Booth escapes.

Rosa Parks

Characters: Rosa Parks, passengers, white man, bus driver

1. An exhausted Rosa Parks boards the bus.
2. At the next stop, more passengers fill the bus seats.
3. A white man boards and demands that Rosa give up her seat.
4. Others move to the back of the bus, but Rosa refuses.
5. Rosa Parks is arrested.

Pocahontas

Characters: John Smith, Powhatan, two men, Pocahontas

1. While John Smith has his head on a stone, Chief Powhatan orders two men to kill him.
2. The two men raise their clubs.
3. Pocahontas shields John Smith.
4. The two men lower the clubs; John Smith is saved.

Civil War Battlefield Amputation

Characters: Orderlies, soldier, doctor, nurses

1. The orderlies deliver the wounded soldier.
2. The doctor, nurses, and orderlies examine the soldier.
3. The doctors and nurses amputate the soldier's arm.
4. The orderlies carry the soldier's body back to the field.

The Battle of Bull Run

Characters: Sightseers, soldiers from the North and the South, Stonewall Jackson

1. Crowds of sightseers arrive with picnic baskets and umbrellas.
2. The fighting begins, although the untrained armies have trouble telling the North from the South.
3. The South, under the leadership of Stonewall Jackson, holds the line and wins the battle.
4. The defeated Union soldiers and the picnickers head back home.

A Glossary of Drama/Theatre Terms

The following terms may be helpful to know and use with your students.

actor's neutral—Actors stand with their weight evenly balanced on both feet, hands by their sides, faces expressionless.

articulate—speak clearly and not too quickly—and to use effective vocal expression.

cheat—to turn the body out toward the audience for better communication of speech and facial expression.

cue—any word or action that signals the beginning of another action or speech.

blackout—a lighting cue that calls for the stage to be totally darkened in a split second.

blocking—the basic movements of the actors, including entrances, exits, and crosses (stage directions meaning to move across the stage from one side to another).

concentration—the actor's focused attention to what's happening at each moment. (Good concentration helps student actors avoid laughter and giggling.)

"Curtain"—This spoken word (generally used in rehearsals) indicates that the dramatic action is about to start. It may also be said to indicate the completion of a scene.

downstage—the part of the stage or playing area closest to the audience.

ensemble playing—working as a team to create a total effect.

focal point—a point of concentration, the spot in the room where actors fix their gaze as if they are looking at a particular sight.

lines of dialogue—the words, sentences, or phrases spoken by actors playing characters.

"Places"—This spoken word is a cue for actors to get ready to begin their scene and (in rehearsals) for observers to give their attention to the actors.

setting –the surroundings in which the dramatic action takes place.

stage left—the playing area to the <u>actor's</u> left.

stage right—the playing area to the <u>actor's</u> right.

subtext—the unspoken meaning of a character's words or actions; a character's thoughts.

upstage—the part of the stage or playing area farthest away from the audience. **Upstaging** refers to any noise or action that takes attention away from the focus of the scene.

voice projection—effective speaking volume; loudness.

Made in the USA
Middletown, DE
01 August 2017